There are all kinds of shops
in the High Street.
This is the fish shop.

Sometimes we go to the supermarket

AT THE SHOPS

Written and illustrated by
Lesley Anne Ivory

LONDON * TORONTO * NEW YORK

First published September 1970
Reprinted September 1974
Reprinted 1982
Reprinted 1984
© Lesley Anne Ivory 1970

All rights reserved. No part of this publication may be reproduced, stored in a retrieval system, or transmitted, in any form or by any means, electronic, mechanical, photocopying, recording or otherwise, without the prior permission of Burke Publishing Company Limited.

ISBN 0222 66900 4 Hardbound
ISBN 0222 66912 8 Softback

Burke Publishing Company Limited
Pegasus House, 116–120 Golden Lane, London EC1Y 0TL, England.
Burke Publishing (Canada) Limited
Registered Office: 20 Queen Street West, Suite 3000
Box 30, Toronto, Canada M5H 1V5.
Burke Publishing Company Inc.
Registered Office: 333 State Street, PO Box 1740
Bridgeport, Connecticut 06601, U.S.A.
Printed in the Netherlands by Deltaprint Holland

to do our shopping.

When we are tired
we go to a café
for a drink.

We have biscuits at the café too.

Yesterday
 the boys went to the barber's shop.
Julian watched James have his hair cut.

In the afternoon
   the girls went shopping with Mummy.

She tried on pretty hats.

On the way home
they looked at
the dresses
in the
shop windows.

Today Mummy took James
   to the shoeshop.
He tried on a pair of new shoes.

When we have money to spend
we go to the sweetshop . . .

. . . the bookshop

. . . or the toyshop.

On Saturday,
we all went to the pet shop.

We bought some goldfish.

Then we went home with our shopping.